HAL•LEONARD

JAZZ PLAY-ALONG®

Book & Audio for B♭, E♭, C and Bass Clef Instruments

VOLUME 4

PLAYBACK+
Speed • Pitch • Balance • Loop

Jazz Ballads
9 Jazz Ballad Classics

Arranged and Produced by
Mark Taylor

TITLE	C Treble Instruments	B♭ Instruments	E♭ Instruments	C Bass Instruments
But Beautiful	4	20	36	52
Here's That Rainy Day	6	22	38	54
Body and Soul	8	24	40	56
Misty	9	25	41	57
My Foolish Heart	10	26	42	58
My Funny Valentine	12	28	44	60
My One and Only Love	14	30	46	62
My Romance	16	32	48	64
The Nearness of You	18	34	50	66
Lyrics				67

To access audio, visit:
www.halleonard.com/mylibrary

5311-3793-5767-3839

T0055406

ISBN 978-0-634-04406-9

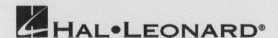

HAL•LEONARD®

World headquarters, contact:
Hal Leonard
7777 West Bluemound Road
Milwaukee, WI 53213
Email: info@halleonard.com

In Europe, contact:
Hal Leonard Europe Limited
1 Red Place
London, W1K 6PL
Email: info@halleonardeurope.com

In Australia, contact:
Hal Leonard Australia Pty. Ltd.
4 Lentara Court
Cheltenham, Victoria, 3192 Australia
Email: info@halleonard.com.au

Jazz Ballads

Volume 4

Arranged and Produced by
Mark Taylor

Featured Players:

Graham Breedlove–Trumpet
John Desalme–Tenor Sax
Tony Nalker–Piano
Jim Roberts–Bass
Steve Fidyk–Drums

HOW TO USE THE AUDIO:

Each song has <u>two</u> tracks:

1) Split Track/Demonstration

Woodwind, **Brass**, **Keyboard**, and **Mallet Players** can use this track as a learning tool for melody style and inflection.

Bass Players can learn and perform with this track – remove the recorded bass track by turning down the volume on the LEFT channel.

Keyboard and **Guitar Players** can learn and perform with this track – remove the recorded piano part by turning down the volume on the RIGHT channel.

2) Backing Track

Soloists or **Groups** can learn and perform with this accompaniment track with the RHYTHM SECTION only.

BUT BEAUTIFUL

WORDS BY JOHNNY BURKE
MUSIC BY JIMMY VAN HEUSEN

C VERSION

HERE'S THAT RAINY DAY

FROM CARNIVAL IN FLANDERS

WORDS BY JOHNNY BURKE
MUSIC BY JIMMY VAN HEUSEN

C VERSION

SOLOS

MOLTO RIT.

BODY AND SOUL

WORDS BY EDWARD HEYMAN,
ROBERT SOUR AND FRANK EYTON
MUSIC BY JOHN GREEN

C VERSION

MISTY

MY FOOLISH HEART

C VERSION

WORDS BY NED WASHINGTON
MUSIC BY VICTOR YOUNG

MY FUNNY VALENTINE

FROM BABES IN ARMS

WORDS BY LORENZ HART
MUSIC BY RICHARD RODGERS

C VERSION

MY ONE AND ONLY LOVE

WORDS BY ROBERT MELLIN
MUSIC BY GUY WOOD

C VERSION

MY ROMANCE

FROM JUMBO

C VERSION

WORDS BY LORENZ HART
MUSIC BY RICHARD RODGERS

THE NEARNESS OF YOU
FROM THE PARAMOUNT PICTURE ROMANCE IN THE DARK

WORDS BY NED WASHINGTON
MUSIC BY HOAGY CARMICHAEL

C VERSION

Bb LEAD SHEETS

BUT BEAUTIFUL

WORDS BY JOHNNY BURKE
MUSIC BY JIMMY VAN HEUSEN

Bb VERSION

HERE'S THAT RAINY DAY

FROM CARNIVAL IN FLANDERS

WORDS BY JOHNNY BURKE
MUSIC BY JIMMY VAN HEUSEN

Bb VERSION

BODY AND SOUL

WORDS BY EDWARD HEYMAN,
ROBERT SOUR AND FRANK EYTON
MUSIC BY JOHN GREEN

MISTY

Bb Version

MUSIC BY ERROLL GARNER

MY FOOLISH HEART

Words by Ned Washington
Music by Victor Young

Bb Version

MY FUNNY VALENTINE

FROM BABES IN ARMS

WORDS BY LORENZ HART
MUSIC BY RICHARD RODGERS

My One and Only Love

WORDS BY ROBERT MELLIN
MUSIC BY GUY WOOD

MY ROMANCE
FROM JUMBO

WORDS BY LORENZ HART
MUSIC BY RICHARD RODGERS

THE NEARNESS OF YOU

FROM THE PARAMOUNT PICTURE ROMANCE IN THE DARK

WORDS BY NED WASHINGTON
MUSIC BY HOAGY CARMICHAEL

Bb VERSION

Eb LEAD SHEETS

BUT BEAUTIFUL

WORDS BY JOHNNY BURKE
MUSIC BY JIMMY VAN HEUSEN

Eb VERSION

HERE'S THAT RAINY DAY

FROM CARNIVAL IN FLANDERS

WORDS BY JOHNNY BURKE
MUSIC BY JIMMY VAN HEUSEN

Eb VERSION

BODY AND SOUL

WORDS BY EDWARD HEYMAN,
ROBERT SOUR AND FRANK EYTON
MUSIC BY JOHN GREEN

Eb VERSION

MISTY

Eb VERSION

MUSIC BY ERROLL GARNER

MY FOOLISH HEART

Words by Ned Washington
Music by Victor Young

Eb Version

MY FUNNY VALENTINE

FROM BABES IN ARMS

WORDS BY LORENZ HART
MUSIC BY RICHARD RODGERS

MY ONE AND ONLY LOVE

WORDS BY ROBERT MELLIN
MUSIC BY GUY WOOD

MY ROMANCE
FROM JUMBO

WORDS BY LORENZ HART
MUSIC BY RICHARD RODGERS

THE NEARNESS OF YOU

FROM THE PARAMOUNT PICTURE ROMANCE IN THE DARK

WORDS BY NED WASHINGTON
MUSIC BY HOAGY CARMICHAEL

E♭ VERSION

𝄢 C LEAD SHEETS

BUT BEAUTIFUL

WORDS BY JOHNNY BURKE
MUSIC BY JIMMY VAN HEUSEN

HERE'S THAT RAINY DAY

FROM CARNIVAL IN FLANDERS

WORDS BY JOHNNY BURKE
MUSIC BY JIMMY VAN HEUSEN

55

BODY AND SOUL

WORDS BY EDWARD HEYMAN,
ROBERT SOUR AND FRANK EYTON
MUSIC BY JOHN GREEN

MISTY

MUSIC BY ERROLL GARNER

MY FOOLISH HEART

Words by Ned Washington
Music by Victor Young

C Version

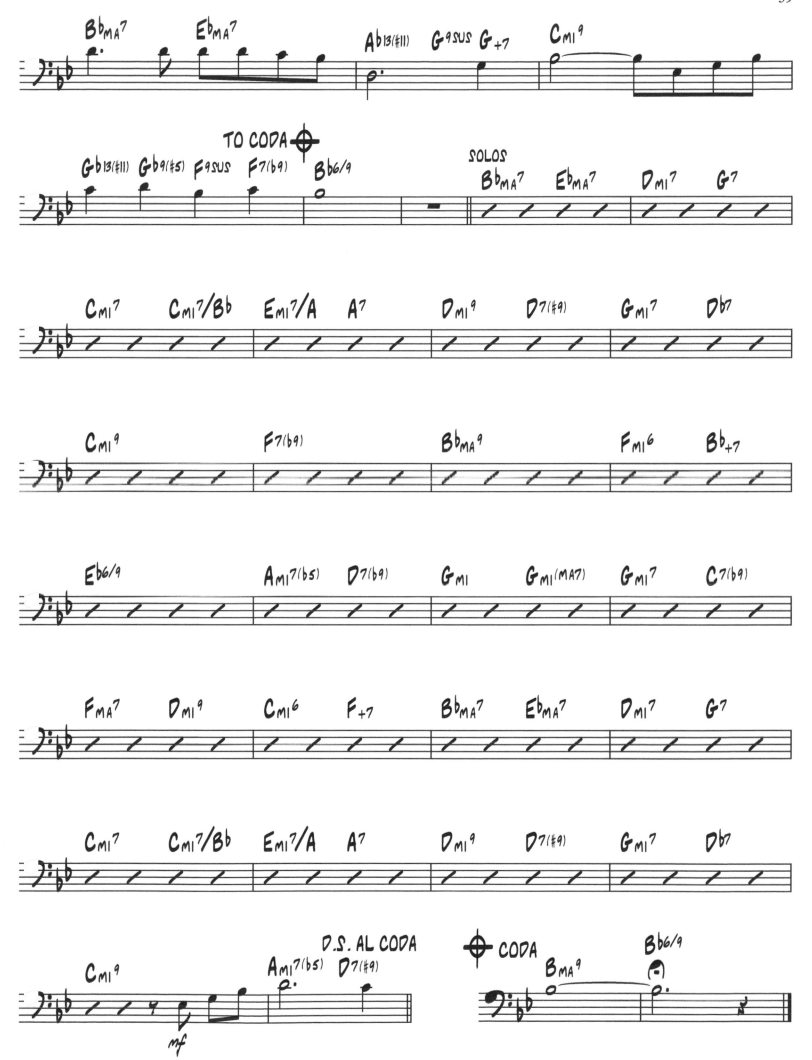

MY FUNNY VALENTINE

FROM BABES IN ARMS

WORDS BY LORENZ HART
MUSIC BY RICHARD RODGERS

MY ONE AND ONLY LOVE

WORDS BY ROBERT MELLIN
MUSIC BY GUY WOOD

MY ROMANCE

FROM JUMBO

WORDS BY LORENZ HART
MUSIC BY RICHARD RODGERS

THE NEARNESS OF YOU

FROM THE PARAMOUNT PICTURE ROMANCE IN THE DARK

WORDS BY NED WASHINGTON
MUSIC BY HOAGY CARMICHAEL

Lyrics

BUT BEAUTIFUL

Love is funny or it's sad,
Or it's quiet or it's mad;
It's a good thing or it's bad,
But beautiful!

Beautiful to take a chance
And if you fall, you fall;
And I'm thinking
I wouldn't mind at all.

Love is tearful or it's gay,
It's a problem or it's play;
It's a heartache either way,
But beautiful!

And I'm thinking if you were mine
I'd never let you go;
And that would be but beautiful
I know.

BODY AND SOUL

My heart is sad and lonely,
For you I sigh, for you, dear, only.
Why haven't you seen it?
I'm all for you, body and soul!

I spend my days in longing
And wond'ring why it's me you're wronging,
I tell you I mean it,
I'm all for you, body and soul!

I can't believe it, it's hard to conceive
That you'd turn away romance.
Are you pretending, it looks like the ending
Unless I could have
One more dance to prove, dear.

My life a wreck you're making,
You know I'm yours for just the taking;
I'd gladly surrender myself to you,
Body and soul!

HERE'S THAT RAINY DAY

Maybe I should have saved those leftover dreams;
Funny, but here's that rainy day.
Here's that rainy day they told me about,
And I laughed at the thought that it might turn out this way.

Where is that worn out wish that I threw aside
After it brought my lover near?
Funny how love becomes a cold rainy day.
Funny that rainy day is here.

MISTY

Look at me,
I'm as helpless as a kitten up a tree
And I feel like I'm clinging to a cloud,
I can't understand,
I get misty just holding your hand.

Walk my way
And a thousand violins begin to play,
Or it might be the sound of your hello,
That music I hear,
I get misty, the moment you're near.

You can say
That you're leading me on,
But it's just what I want you to do,
Don't you notice
How hopelessly I'm lost,
That's why I'm following you.

On my own,
Would I wander through
This wonderland alone,
Never knowing my right foot from my left,
My hat from my glove,
I'm too misty and too much in love.

MY FOOLISH HEART

The night is like a lovely tune,
Beware my foolish heart!
How white the ever constant moon;
Take care my foolish heart!

There's a line between
Love and fascination
That's hard to see
On an evening such as this,
For they both give
The very same sensation
When you're lost
In the magic of a kiss.

His lips are much too close to mine,
Beware my foolish heart!
But should our eager lips combine
Then let the fire start!

For this time it isn't fascination,
Or a dream that will fade
And fall apart,
It's love this time,
It's love, my foolish heart.

MY FUNNY VALENTINE

My funny Valentine,
Sweet comic Valentine,
You make me smile with my heart.
Your looks are laughable,
Unphotographable,
Yet you're my fav'rite work of art.

Is your figure less than Greek;
Is your mouth a little weak,
When you open it to speak,
Are you smart?

But don't change a hair for me,
Not if you care for me,
Stay, little Valentine, stay!
Each day is Valentine's Day.

MY ONE AND ONLY LOVE

The very thought of you
Makes my heart sing
Like an April breeze
On the wings of spring.
And you appear in all your splendor,
My one and only love.

The shadows fall
And spread their mystic charms
In the hush of night
While you're in my arms.
I feel your lips so warm and tender,
My one and only love.

The touch of your hand is like heaven,
A heaven that I've never known.
The blush on your cheek
Whenever I speak
Tells me that you are my own.

You fill my eager heart with such desire.
Ev'ry kiss you give sets my soul on fire.
I give myself in sweet surrender,
My one and only love.

MY ROMANCE

My romance doesn't have
To have a moon in the sky.
My romance doesn't need
A blue lagoon standing by.
No month of May, no twinkling stars,
No hide away, no soft guitars.

My romance doesn't need
A castle rising in Spain
Nor a dance to a
Constantly surprising refrain.
Wide awake I can make my most
Fantastic dreams come true.
My romance doesn't need a thing
But you.

THE NEARNESS OF YOU

It's not the pale mood that excites me,
That thrills and delights me.
Oh, no it's just the nearness of you.

It isn't your sweet conversation
That brings this sensation.
Oh, no it's just the nearness of you.

When you're in my arms
And I feel you so close to me,
All my wildest dreams come true.

I need no soft lights to enchant me
If you'll only grant me the right
To hold you ever so tight,
And to feel in the night
The nearness of you.

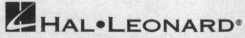